THE DELICIOSA MEXICAN COOKBOOK - Quick and Easy Mexican Recipes

Spice Up Your Life with Authentic Mexican Food

Are you bored of eating the same pizzas, burgers, steaks and cakes? How about trying some authentic Mexican food?

Mexican food is irresistibly delectable in its true form. If you ever tried Mexican food and you didn't like it, it means it wasn't Authentic. Mexican food is very common these days and almost every age group likes it. However not everyone is able to follow the authentic Mexican recipes. A lot of people modify the recipes as per the contemporary taste. Well this book is surely not going to do that

The recipes contained in this book are truly Mexican, no jumbling of flavors. So why have impure Mexican food when you can have authentic and even more delicious at your home.

The **Deliciosa Mexican Cookbook** contains the following:

1. Recipes for a variety of Tacos and Enchiladas.

2. Recipes for Mexican dips and appetizers

3. Authentic recipes of some Mexican specialty main course items, including recipes for both, vegetarians and meat lovers.

4. Quick and easy recipes for Mexican drinks and desserts.

5. Cooking time, serving size and nutritional facts along with every recipe.

So just go ahead and try out a few and experience the real Mexican Flavors!

Contents

Mexican Dips and Appetizers

Authentic Mexican Salsa

SERVES 16

Cooking Time: 5 minutes

Nutritional Facts: Calories 22.5, Protein 0.9 g, Total Fat 0.3 g, Carbohydrates 6 g

Ingredients

> 4 jalapenos, chopped
>
> 6 large tomatoes
>
> 1 tsp of minced garlic
>
> 1 avocado, peeled and chopped
>
> Half bunch of cilantro, chopped
>
> 1 tsp of salt
>
> 1 cucumber, peeled and chopped (optional)
>
> 2 medium sized onions, chopped
>
> Juice of 1 lemon

Preparation Method

Place whole tomatoes in a skillet.

Roast over medium-high flame, till the skin of the tomatoes begin to crack.

Let the tomatoes cool for a while and then chop them finely.

Combine the roasted chopped tomatoes with all the other ingredients in large bowl.

Mix well and serve!

Mexican Bean Hummus

SERVES 16

Cooking Time: 5 – 7 minutes

Nutritional Facts: Calories 33, Protein 1.7 g, Total Fat 0.7 g, Carbohydrates 5.3 g

Ingredients

2 Tbsp chopped fresh cilantro

3 cups black beans (home cooked or canned)

2 Tbsp ground cumin

¼ cup vegetable broth

½ green pepper, chopped

1 ½ tsp olive oil

1 small onion, chopped

3 cloves of garlic, minced

Preparation Method

If you are using canned beans, rinse and drain them.

Put the olive oil in a skillet and heat it over medium-high flame.

When the oil is hot, put onions, garlic and pepper in it.

Sauté for about 3 minutes, till the onions starts to brown. Stir in cumin.

Reduce the flame to medium and cook for 2 more minutes, while stirring constantly.

Put the beans in a food processor. Pulse a couple of times.

Add the sautéed vegetables to the processor and pulse a few more times.

Start adding the vegetable broth to the food processor, spoon by spoon while the processor is running. Keep adding the broth till the dip reaches the desired consistency.

Drizzle with fresh cilantro and serve!

This sauce can be stored in the refrigerator for up to ten days.

Vegan Taco Bean Salad

SERVES 5 – 6

Cooking Time: 10 minutes

Nutritional Facts: Calories 395, Protein 14 g, Total Fat 17 g, Carbohydrates 52 g

Ingredients

2 cups shredded romaine lettuce or iceberg

1 ½ cups long grain brown rice (cooked)

1 ½ cups corn kernels (fresh)

1/3 cup prepared salsa

1 can of black beans (15 oz.), rinsed, (substitute: kidney beans)

1 large sized onion, diced

1 Tbsp of chili powder

2 Tbsp olive oil

4 large tomatoes

Half cup fresh cilantro, chopped

1 ½ tsp of dried oregano, divided

1 cup of Pepper Jack Cheese (shredded), divided

¼ tsp of salt

2 ½ cups tortilla chips (roughly crumbled)

Preparation Method

Put the olive oil into a nonstick skillet and heat it over medium flame.

When the oil is hot, add onions and corns to it.

Sauté till the onions starts to brown; this should take approximately 5 minutes.

Now dice one tomato coarsely and put it in the same skillet. Stir to mix.

Stir in the beans, rice, 1 tsp oregano, chili powder and salt.

Cook for 5 minutes while stirring frequently. Remove the skillet off the heat.

Now roughly dice the remaining tomatoes and place them in bowl along with salsa, cilantro and the leftover oregano. Mix well and set aside.

Combine the lettuce and bean-rice mixture in the serving plate.

Stir in half of the tomato-oregano mixture along with two-third cup of the cheese. Mix well.

Garnish with the remaining tomato-oregano mixture and cheese.

Finally, sprinkle the crumbled tortilla over the salad and serve!

Flavorful Mole Sauce

SERVES 10

Cooking Time: 40 – 45 minutes

Nutritional Facts: Calories 42.3, Protein 2.1 g, Total Fat 0.1 g, Carbohydrates 8.6 g

Ingredients

2 cups chicken broth

3 white onions, cut into quarters

1 tsp chili powder

3 cloves of garlic, peeled

3 ancho chilies, dried

1 tsp cocoa powder (unsweetened)

4 plum tomatoes, cut into quarters

2 banana peppers

Zest of 1 lime

1 lime, juiced

Preparation Method

Adjust the oven rack to the highest slot.

Preheat the oven to broil.

Combine onion, tomatoes, banana peppers and garlic in a cast iron skillet.

Put the skillet under the broiler.

Let it cook till the tomatoes starts to blacken, while stirring all the vegetables once in between.

Carefully remove the skillet from the oven and set aside to cool for at least 5 minutes.

Fill a large bowl with water and soak the chilies in it for 10 minutes.

Remove the stems from the ancho chilies.

Combine the soaked chilies along with the cooked vegetables in a food processor.

Pulse all the vegetables are thoroughly blended and smooth.

Transfer the blended mixture to a saucepan.

Stir in the chili powder, cocoa powder and chicken broth.

Cook over medium flame for 25 minutes.

Remove the saucepan off the heat.

Finally, stir in the lime juice and zest.

Serve!

Spicy Veggie and Tofu Soup

SERVES 8

Cooking Time: 60 minutes

Nutritional Facts: Calories 208, Protein 7 g, Total Fat 13 g, Carbohydrates 18 g

Ingredients

>1 large sized avocado (ripe), cut into ¼ inch cubes
>
>4 cups vegetable broth
>
>3 large dried pasilla chiles
>
>¾ cup shredded Mexican melting cheese
>
>1 medium sized white onion, cut into ¼ thick slices
>
>1 large sprig of epazote
>
>2 Tbsp canola oil
>
>3 cloves of garlic, peeled
>
>4 cups chopped chard (substitute: chopped kale)
>
>1 (15 oz.) can of fire-roasted diced tomatoes with liquid
>
>2 tsp extra virgin olive oil
>
>4 cups water
>
>½ tsp salt
>
>14 oz. extra firm tofu, drain, rinsed, pat dry and cut into half inch cubes.
>
>2 cups coarsely broken tortilla chips

Preparation Method

Hold the chiles with metal tongs and toast them an inch above open flame.

Toast one side for a few seconds, flip and toast again till the kitchen is filled with its aroma.

One by one, toast all the three chiles in the same way.

Allow the toasted chiles to cool for a bit.

When the chiles are cool enough to hold, remove its stems and seeds.

Break the chiles into random pieces and place them in a food processor.

Pour the can of tomatoes in the processor along with the liquid.

Pulse till the ingredients and blended and mixed.

Now place a Dutch oven medium flame and heat 2 Tbsp canola oil in it.

When the oil is hot, add onion and garlic to it.

Sauté for 7 – 9 minutes, till the onion is golden.

Scoop up the garlic and onion with a slotted spoon and put them in the food processor containing the tomato-chile mixture. Keep the Dutch oven on.

Pulse till it becomes a smooth mixture.

Return the entire blended mixture to the Dutch oven.

Cook for about 6 minutes or till attains the consistency of tomato paste, while stirring constantly.

Stir in water, broth and epazote.

Bring it to a boil. After the first boil, reduce the heat to simmer.

While it is simmering, take another skillet and add the 2 tsp olive oil in it.

Heat the olive oil over medium flame.

When the oil is hot, add tofu in it.

Cook the tofu till it starts to brown, 6 – 8 minutes. Stir after every 2 minutes.

Add the browned tofu to the simmering soup in the Dutch oven.

Stir in chard and salt in the soup.

Cook while stirring, till the chard is wilted, for about 2 minutes.

Pour the soup in serving bowls.

Garnish each serving with avocado, tortilla chips and cheese.

Serve it hot!

Mexican Habanero Pickle Veggies

SERVES 7 – 8

Cooking Time: 30 minutes

Nutritional Facts: Calories 116, Protein 1 g, Total Fat 10 g, Carbohydrates 7 g

Ingredients

1 large head of cauliflower, break into small florets

1 Tbsp black peppercorns

1 cup extra virgin olive oil

1 yellow or red bell pepper

2 tsp coriander seeds

2 ½ cups distilled white vinegar

1 medium sized onion, cut into thin slices

2 tsp allspice berries

6 bay leaves

1 tsp whole cloves

1 lb. fresh pearl onions, peeled

1 tsp cumin seeds

10 cloves of garlic, peeled

2 Tbsp dried oregano

3 medium sized carrots, cut into ¼ inch slices

1 small habanero pepper, remove the stems and cut into thin slices

1 Tbsp salt

Preparation Method

Cut the bell pepper lengthwise into ¼ inch slices. Set aside.

Now first you need an 8-inch square double layer of cheesecloth.

Put allspice berries, cloves, coriander seeds and peppercorns in the center of the cloth.

Gather the edges and tie them securely to enclose the spices in the cheesecloth.

Put the olive oil in a Dutch oven and heat it over medium heat.

Sauté the onion slices and garlic in it for 5 minutes.

Stir in pearl onion, carrots, habareno, cauliflower and bell pepper.

Cook for 7 – 9 minutes, till the vegetable are tender yet crispy. Stir occasionally.

Add vinegar, oregano, cumin, salt, bay leaves and the cheesecloth bag to the vegetables.

Cook for 2 more minutes.

Turn off the heat and let it rest for 15 minutes.

Transfer all of it to a large nonreactive bowl.

Put it in the refrigerator for 2 hours. Stir after every 30 minutes.

The spicy delicious pickle is ready!

Quick and Easy Tortilla Chips

SERVES 12

Cooking Time: 15 – 20 minutes

Nutritional Facts: Calories 142, Protein 2 g, Total Fat 2 g, Carbohydrates 29 g

Ingredients

> 1 tsp chili powder
>
> 24 corn tortillas (6 inch each)
>
> 5 Tbsp lime juice
>
> Cooking spray of canola oil
>
> ½ tsp salt

Preparation Method

Position one oven rack in the lower third and another rack in the middle of the oven

Now set the oven to preheat at 375°F.

Thoroughly coat all the tortillas with cooking spray. Make sure you coat both the sides of the tortillas.

Cut the tortillas into quarters.

Take 2 baking sheets and arrange a single layer of tortillas each sheet. Do not overlap the tortillas. Bake in batches if necessary.

Take a small bowl and combine chili powder and lime juice in it.

Brush the lime-chili mixture on the tortillas.

Sprinkle salt over the tortillas.

Put one sheet in the middle rack and another in the lower third of the oven.

Bake for 15 – 20 minutes, till the tortillas are crispy and golden. Switch the position of the sheets once in between.

Authentic Mexican Roasted Guacamole

MAKES 4 cups (about 16 servings)

Cooking Time: 15 minutes

Nutritional Facts: Calories 310, Protein 7 g, Total Fat 21 g, Carbohydrates 28 g

Ingredients

>6 ripe avocados
>
>2 Tbsp fresh lime juice
>
>6 cloves of garlic, unpeeled
>
>Half cup fresh cilantro, chopped
>
>1 tsp salt

Preparation Method

Put the unpeeled garlic cloves in a pan over medium flame.

Cook for 10 – 15 minutes, till it is soft and attain black spots while turning occasionally.

When the garlic is cool enough to handle, peel off its skin and chop finely.

Scoop out the avocado flesh in a bowl.

Stir in lime juice, garlic and salt. Mash and mix everything,

Stir in salt.

Plastic wrap the bowl and put it in the refrigerator till it is ready to serve.

Butternut Veggie Soup

SERVES 9 – 10

Cooking Time: 1 hour and 30 minutes

Nutritional Facts: Calories 55, Protein 2 g, Total Fat 1 g, Carbohydrates 10 g

Ingredients

Half cup plain yogurt (nonfat)

1 ½ lbs. pounds butternut squash

½ tsp ground chipotle pepper

1 carrot, diced

¼ tsp freshly ground black pepper

2 stalks of celery, diced

1 tsp canola oil

1 small sized onion, diced

6 cups vegetable broth

1 tsp ground cumin

1 tsp sea salt

1/8 tsp ground cloves

2 Tbsp chopped parsley

Preparation Method

Set the oven to preheat at 350°F.

Cut the butternut squash in half and remove the seeds.

Place the halves, cut side down, on a baking sheet.

Put it in the oven for 45 – 60 minutes, till the squash is tender when a knife is pierced into it.

Scoop out its flesh in a bowl. Set aside to cool.

Put the canola oil in a saucepan and heat it over medium flame.

Combine onion, celery and carrots in the saucepan. Stir to mix.

Increase the flame to medium-high, cover the saucepan and let it cook for 10 minutes or till the veggies are soft. Stir occasionally.

Add the squash flesh, cloves, chipotle and cumin to the saucepan. Mix well.

Stir in the broth.

Cover the saucepan again and let it simmer for 20 – 25 minutes.

Transfer the puree to a food processor and blend till it becomes a smooth puree. Do it in batches if necessary. Alternatively, you can also run an immersion blender in the saucepan.

Season the soup with salt and pepper.

Ladle the soup into serving bowls.

Garnish each serving with a dollop of yoghurt.

Sprinkle parsley over the soup and serve!

Slow Cooker Enchilada Soup

SERVES 8

Cooking Time: 4 – 8 minutes

Nutritional Facts: Calories 169, Protein 17.4 g, Total Fat 2.5 g, Carbohydrates 20.3 g

Ingredients

>   3 cans of chicken broth (14.5 oz. per can)
>
>   1 lb. frozen shredded chicken
>
>   1 can (15 oz.) of black beans, rinsed
>
>   1 can (4 oz.) of chopped green chile peppers
>
>   1 tsp cumin
>
>   1 can (10 oz.) of enchilada sauce
>
>   1 medium sized onion, diced
>
>   2 cloves of garlic, minced
>
>   1 can (15 oz.) of whole peeled tomatoes, mashed
>
>   10 oz. frozen corn
>
>   ¼ tsp ground black pepper

Preparation Method

Combine the chicken, enchilada sauce, green chiles, onion, tomatoes and garlic in a slow cooker. Mix well.

Stir in the broth, salt, pepper, corns, cumin and black beans.

Cover the cooker and let it cook on low heat for 7 – 8 hours or on high heat for 4 hours.

Serve it hot!

Spicy Cheesy Sweet Potatoes

SERVES 6

Cooking Time: 30 minutes

Nutritional Facts: Calories 140, Protein 5.5 g, Total Fat 4.2 g, Carbohydrates 21 g

Ingredients

3 large sweet potatoes (about 5 inches long), peeled and thinly sliced

Half cup shredded sharp Cheddar

1 Tbsp ground cumin

3 cloves of garlic, chopped

¾ cup skim milk

½ tsp ground black pepper

1 large sized white onion, thinly sliced

1 tsp hot sauce

1 tsp ground coriander

Nonstick cooking spray

Preparation Method

Set the oven to preheat at 400ºF.

Combine the coriander, cumin and pepper in small bowl. Set aside.

Coat a casserole dish with cooking spray.

Arrange an even layer of half of the sweet potato slices in the greased dish.

Sprinkle one-third of the spice mixture over the sweet potatoes.

Spread the onions over it followed by chopped garlic.

Sprinkle another one-third of the spice mixture.

Arrange the second layer of the sweet potatoes.

Sprinkle the remaining spice mixture.

Pour milk over it followed by hot sauce.

Finally, spread the cheese over it.

Cover the dish and bake for 20 minutes, then bake uncovered for another 10 minutes or till the cheese starts to brown.

Enjoy!

Variety of Mexican Tacos

Cheesilicious Breakfast Tacos

MAKES about 8 tacos

Cooking Time: 10 – 15 minutes

Nutritional Facts: Calories 238, Protein 8.8 g, Total Fat 17.3 g, Carbohydrates 12.3 g

Ingredients

> 2 Tbsp butter
>
> 4 large eggs
>
> 1 cup Monterey Jack cheese with jalapeno peppers (shredded)
>
> ¼ cup sliced green onions (substitute: diced green bell pepper)
>
> 8 taco shells
>
> 18 oz. creamy three cheese cooking sauce, divided

Preparation Method

Combine eggs and ¾ of the three cheese cooking sauce in a bowl. Whisk well.

Whisk in the sliced green onions.

Put butter in a nonstick skillet and heat it over medium heat.

Pour the egg mixture into skillet.

Cook just like you make an egg scramble, for about 4 minutes or till the eggs are thickened yet succulent.

Heat the taco shells.

Spoon about ¼ cup of egg mixture and 2 Tbsp shredded cheese into each shell.

Serve with salsa.

Authentic Taqueria Style Tacos

SERVES 8

Cooking Time: About 60 minutes

Nutritional Facts: Calories 369, Protein 18 g, Total Fat 19.7 g, Carbohydrates 32 g

Ingredients

¼ cup fresh cilantro, chopped

1 ½ Tbsp fresh lime juice, divided

1 ½ lbs flank steak

1 small white onion, diced

1 small white onion, cut into quarters

4 cloves garlic, peeled

2 cloves of garlic, minced

½ tsp freshly ground black pepper

¼ cup soy sauce

1 large tomato, diced

3 Tbsp white vinegar

Half cup olive oil

½ tsp dried oregano

1 cups grated cotija cheese

½ tsp salt

½ tsp chili powder

½ tsp ground white pepper

½ tsp ground cumin

½ tsp paprika

½ tsp garlic powder

2 dried New Mexico chile pods

1 jalapeno pepper, diced

16 corn tortillas

Preparation Method

Place the steak in a large baking dish.

Take a bowl and add in it the vinegar, 1 tablespoon lime juice, soy sauce, minced garlic, olive oil, salt, white pepper, black pepper, oregano, garlic powder, paprika, chili powder and cumin. Mix well.

Pour this mixture over the steak in the baking dish.

Toss the steak to coat it with the spice mixture.

Cover the dish with a plastic wrap and marinate for at least 1 hour (maximum 8 hours).

Now take a small bowl and combine in it the cilantro, the diced white onion and remaining lime juice. Set aside.

Place a skillet over medium-high flame.

When the skillet is hot, put the chile pods in it. Toast for a few minutes.

Transfer the toasted pods to a bowl filled with water.

Soak the pods for 30 minutes.

Meanwhile, set the oven to preheat at 450oF.

Take another baking sheet and place tomatoes, the white onion quarters, whole peeled garlic cloves and jalapenos over it. Mix well.

Put it in the oven for 20 minutes, or till the veggies are toasted but not scorched.

Transfer the roasted vegetables to a food processor, along with a bit more salt and pepper if you want.

Drain the soaked chili pods and add them to the food processor.

Pulse till it becomes a smooth puree.

Now take another large skillet and heat oil in it over medium-high flame.

Cut the marinated steak into small cubes or thin strips.

Put the meat in the skillet and cook till the meat is cooked through and almost all the liquid evaporates. Stir constantly while cooking.

Now one by one warm up the tortillas in a nonstick skillet. It will take just about a minute per side to make the tortillas warm and pliable. You can also do this in a microwave oven.

Arrange two tortillas on each serving plate.

Spoon a generous portion of beef on each followed by a sprinkle of onion relish.

Top each serving with a large tablespoon of roasted vegetable puree.

Finally, sprinkle cheese over it and serve!

Cheese and Sausage Burritos

SERVES 8

Cooking Time: 15 – 25 minutes

Nutritional Facts: Calories 822, Protein 39.5 g, Total Fat 53.7 g, Carbohydrates 43 g

Ingredients

1 ½ lbs chorizo sausage, remove the casings and crumble the sausages

8 flour tortillas

2 green chile peppers, seeded and chopped

2 cups shredded Cheddar cheese

1 cup diced red onion

8 eggs, beaten

Cooking spray

Preparation Method

Coat a large skillet or frying pan with cooking spray. Place it over medium-high heat.

Put the sausages in the coated pan. Cook till the sausages are browned and well crumbled, while stirring constantly.

Stir in the chile pepper and onion. Cook and stir till the onion is soft.

Stir in the beaten eggs.

Reduce the flame to medium-low. Cook and stir till the eggs are well cooked and scrambled.

Warm the tortillas one by one in a nonstick skillet. It will take just about a minute per side to make the tortillas warm and pliable. You can also microwave them for about 30 seconds.

Spoon the chorizo mixture in the centre of each tortilla.

Sprinkle generous amount of cheese over each serving.

Roll it up like a burrito and serve!

Bison Tacos with Sweet and Spicy Salsa

SERVES 5 – 6

Cooking Time: 15 – 20 minutes

Nutritional Facts: Calories 369, Protein 26.3 g, Total Fat 17.4 g, Carbohydrates 26.7 g

Ingredients for Tacos

6 eggs

1 lb ground bison

¼ tsp ground coriander

1 tsp ground cumin

12 corn taco shells, warmed as per the package instructions

Pinch of cayenne pepper

¾ cup shredded Cheddar cheese

Half cup diced onion

½ tsp salt

¼ cup milk

2 Tbsp water

Ingredients for Pineapple Salsa

1/3 cup chopped bell pepper (preferably red)

2 Tbsp fresh lime juice

1 cup chopped fresh pineapple

¼ cup diced red onion

¼ tsp of salt

2 Tbsp fresh cilantro, chopped

1 fresh jalapeno chile pepper, seeded and finely diced

Preparation Method

To make the pineapple salsa,

Combine all the pineapple salsa ingredients in a large bowl.

Mix well and set aside.

To make the tacos,

Place a nonstick skillet over medium-high flame.

Combine bison and onion in the skillet.

Cook and stir till the bison is brown and onion is soft.

Drain off the excess fat.

Stir in the salt, water, cumin, cayenne pepper and coriander.

Cook for another 2 minutes while stirring constantly.

Take a medium bowl and crack all the eggs in it. Whisk well.

Stir in the beaten eggs to the bison mixture. Cook and stir till the egg is cooked and scrambled, about 2 minutes.

Divide the bison mixture evenly between the warmed taco shells.

Top it up with cheese.

Serve with pineapple salsa.

Simple Sirloin Tacos

MAKES 9 tacos

Cooking Time: 10 – 15 minutes

Nutritional Facts: Calories 379, Protein 20 g, Total Fat 21.4 g, Carbohydrates 28 g

Ingredients

> 1 lb. top sirloin steak, cut the steak into thin strips
>
> 9 corn tortillas (6 inch each)
>
> 2 fresh jalapeno peppers, seeded and diced
>
> 2 fl oz. vegetable oil (about 4 Tbsp)
>
> 1 small onion, chopped
>
> Salt to taste
>
> 2 limes, cut into wedges
>
> Half bunch of fresh cilantro, chopped
>
> Freshly ground black pepper to taste

Preparation Method

In a nonstick skillet, heat the vegetable oil over medium-high flame.

Put the steak strips in it. Cook and stir for about 5 minutes, till the steak is cooked through and brown but not too firm.

Drizzle with salt and pepper.

Transfer it to a plate.

Now heat oil in skillet. Fry the tortillas in it one by one for about 30 seconds per side, or till it is brown on both sides.

Place the tortillas on the serving plates.

Spoon equal portions of steak strip mixture over each tortilla.

Top up each serving with onion, cilantro and jalapeño.

Squeeze a bit of lime juice over each serving.

Wrap it up and serve.

Chorizo Cheese Tacos

SERVES 8

Cooking Time: 20 minutes

Nutritional Facts: Calories 537, Protein 30.6 g, Total Fat 34 g, Carbohydrates 27.7 g

Ingredients

1 cup shredded Monterey Jack cheese

12 oz. chorizo sausage

1 tsp pepper

12 eggs

Hot pepper sauce, to taste

1 tsp salt

16 corn tortillas (6 inch each)

Half cup milk

1 cup salsa

Cooking spray

Preparation Method

Place a nonstick skillet over medium-high flame.

Put the sausage in the skillet and crumble it.

Cook and stir till the sausage is brown. Set aside.

Take another skillet and coat it with cooking spray. Place it over medium heat.

Crack all the eggs in a large bowl. Whisk well.

Whisk in the salt and pepper.

Pour the beaten eggs in the skillet. Cook and stir till the eggs are cooked and slightly firm.

Stir in the crumbled sausage. Cook a few more minutes till the eggs are thoroughly mixed in the sausage and firm. Set aside.

Now take another skillet and place it over high flame.

Warm the tortillas in it for about 45 seconds each side, till the tortillas are crispy yet pliable.

Arrange the tortillas on the serving plates.

Sprinkle a bit of cheese over each tortilla.

Top up each serving with hot crumbled sausage mixture, followed by a sprinkle of hot pepper sauce and salsa.

Butternut Tacos with Jalapeno Salsa

MAKES 8 Tacos (about 4 servings)

Cooking Time: 40 – 50 minutes

Nutritional Facts: Calories 406, Protein 13 g, Total Fat 9 g, Carbohydrates 70 g

Ingredients for Butternut Tacos

> 2 cups cooked pinto beans, drained
>
> 4 cups butternut squash (peeled and chopped)
>
> ¼ tsp cumin seeds
>
> ¾ tsp Mexican dried oregano, divided
>
> ½ tsp chili powder
>
> 2 cloves of garlic, smashed unpeeled
>
> ½ tsp salt, divided
>
> 8 corn tortillas (6 inch each)
>
> 4 small dried red chiles, snipped using kitchen shears
>
> 1 Tbsp of olive oil
>
> Half cup finely shredded green or red cabbage
>
> ½ tsp ground cumin (toasted), divided
>
> 8 tsp crumbled queso fresco (substitute: feta cheese)
>
> Half cup fresh cilantro leaves
>
> Freshly ground black pepper to taste

Ingredients for Jalapeno Salsa

> 8 oz. tomatillos, husks removed and rinsed
>
> ½ avocado, ripe and chopped
>
> 1 jalapeno pepper
>
> 3 Tbsp cilantro (fresh)

¼ tsp worth of salt

2 cloves of garlic

¼ cup sliced white onion

Fresh ground pepper

Preparation Method

To make the salsa,

Fill a saucepan with water and bring it to a slow boil.

After the first boil, put the tomatillos in. Let boil for about 7 minutes, till the tomatillos are soft.

Place a nonstick skillet over medium-high flame. Do not put oil in it.

Toast the jalapeno, garlic cloves and onion the skillet.

Cook for 5 – 7 minutes, till the veggies are brown and soft, while turning occasionally.

Allow the veggies to cool a bit.

When the roasted vegetables are cool enough, peel the cloves of garlic.

Now remove the stems and seeds of the jalapeno.

Put the roasted jalapeno, garlic, onion, avocado and boiled tomatillos in a food processor.

Pulse till smooth. Take it out in a bowl.

Stir in the salt, pepper and cilantro. The jalapeno salsa is ready.

To make the tacos,

Set the oven to preheat at 400°F.

Combine the squash and snipped chiles in a bowl. Mix well.

Stir in oil, ¼ tsp of salt, garlic cloves, cumin seeds and ½ tsp oregano. Stir to coat the squash with the spices.

Arrange the seasoned squash in single layer onto a baking tray.

Put it in the oven for about 25 minutes, till it is soft and starts to brown.

Pick out the garlic, peel it, chop it and return it to the squash mixture.

Now take another saucepan and place the beans in it.

Add the remaining oregano, remaining salt, chili powder, ground cumin and pepper to the beans.

Cook over low-medium flame for 10 minutes.

Now one by one, warm the tortillas in a nonstick skillet. It will take just about a minute per side to make the tortillas warm and pliable. You can also microwave them for about 30 seconds.

Spoon about ¼ cup of the bean mixture on each warm tortilla.

Next, spoon equal amount of the butternut squash over the beans.

Top each serving with a sprinkle of cilantro, shredded cabbage, half cup jalapeno salsa and cheese.

Enjoy!

Fajita Tacos

SERVES 6

Cooking Time: 20 – 25 minutes

Nutritional Facts: Calories 395, Protein 23 g, Total Fat 20 g, Carbohydrates 33 g

Ingredients

> 3 poblano peppers
>
> 2 ripe avocados, pitted
>
> ½ tsp freshly ground pepper, divided
>
> 1 lb skirt steak, trimmed
>
> 3 Tbsp fresh lime juice, divided
>
> 1 tsp ground ancho chile,
>
> 2 bunches scallions, trimmed
>
> Half cup chopped fresh cilantro
>
> ½ tsp ground cumin
>
> 1 ½ tsp kosher salt, divided
>
> 3 tsp extra virgin olive oil, divided
>
> 12 corn tortillas (6-inch each), warmed according to package instructions

Preparation Method

Set the grill to preheat at high.

Place the avocados in bowl and mash them with a fork or potato masher.

Add cilantro, ¾ tsp salt, 2 Tbsp lime juice and ¼ tsp pepper to the avocados. Set aside.

Now combine the cumin, ancho chili and the remaining salt and pepper in small bowl.

Brush both sides of the steak with 1 tsp oil and the ancho chili mixture. Let rest.

Brush the poblanos with 1 tsp oil. Set aside.

Brush the scallions with the remaining 1 tsp oil. Set aside

Now grease the grill with cooking spray or any other oil.

Grill the poblanos while turning it often for 8 – 12 minutes, till the poblanos are soft and charred.

Take the poblanos out in a bowl. Cover the bowl and let it sit.

Now grill the scallions while turning frequently for 2 – 4 minutes, till the poblanos are soft and slightly charred. Take them out in a bowl. Set aside.

Now grill the steak for 2 – 3 minutes per side, till it is medium-rare.

Transfer the grilled steak to a cutting board. Cover it with foil and let rest.

When the scallions are cool enough to handle, cut them into 1-inch slices and set them on the serving dish. Add the remaining lime juice and the remaining salt to the scallions, toss to mix. You can also do this in a separate bowl and then place them on the serving dish.

Now take the grilled poblano peppers, peel them, remove the stems and seeds and cut into half inch strips. Place them next to the scallions in the serving dish.

When the steak is cool enough to handle, chop it into small chunks. Arrange the steak chunks on the serving dish along with the mashed avocado mixture and warmed tortillas.

Enjoy!

Sweet Shrimp Tacos

SERVES 8

Cooking Time: 15 minutes

Nutritional Facts: Calories 468, Protein 42 g, Total Fat 7.3 g, Carbohydrates 58.5 g

Ingredients

16 tortillas (6-inch each), warmed according to the package instructions

2 tsp vegetable oil

8 Tbsp honey

2 jalapeno peppers

4 bell peppers, cut into strips

4 tsp ground cumin

2 lbs cocktail shrimp (tails removed), precooked

2 large onions, cut into strips

4 tsp ground coriander

7 cloves of garlic, diced

6 Tbsp chopped fresh cilantro

Salt to taste

Freshly ground black pepper to taste

Preparation Method

Place a nonstick skillet over medium-high flame and heat oil in it.

When the oil is hot, add onions, bell peppers, garlic and jalapeno to it. Sauté for 5 – 10 minutes, till the onions are translucent.

Stir in the precooked shrimps. Heat through.

Drain the excess water out of skillet.

Reduce the flame to low. Stir in the ground coriander, cumin, salt and pepper.

Cook for 30 more seconds, Turn off the heat.

Combine honey and chopped cilantro in a bowl.

Arrange the tortillas in the serving plates.

Spoon equal portions of shrimp over each tortilla.

Drizzle each serving with a spoonful of honey.

Enjoy!

Mexican Enchiladas for All Mealtimes

Queso Fresco Enchiladas

SERVES 6

Cooking Time: 20 minutes

Nutritional Facts: Calories 477, Protein 21 g, Total Fat 24.3 g, Carbohydrates 46 g

Ingredients

3 cups crumbled queso fresco

6 dried chile de arbol peppers, tops slashed

1 cup vegetable oil, for frying

1 cup sour cream

1 tsp salt

18 corn tortillas (6 inch each)

2 medium sized tomatoes, cut into thin slices

¾ cup water

Half cup diced green onions

1 clove of garlic

1 cup shredded lettuce

Preparation Method

Place the dried chilies in a saucepan.

Fill the saucepan with water enough to cover the chilies.

Bring it to boil over medium flame, then reduce the heat to simmer.

Simmer for 15 minutes.

Drain the water and transfer the chilies to a food processor along with the garlic clove and salt.

Pulse till it becomes a smooth puree.

Pass the sauce through the sieve into a plate. Discard the residues.

Now place a nonstick pan over medium flame and heat the oil in it.

Soak each tortilla in the sauce and then place it immediately in the hot oil.

Turn over the tortilla over almost immediately. Cook the other side for 5 seconds and then take it out on a plate lined with paper towel.

Likewise fry all the tortillas, stacking one over the other till all are done.

Spoon about 2 Tbsp queso fresco in the center of each tortilla. Roll it up. If you want to make individual servings, put 3 rolls on each plate.

Top up each serving with a dollop of sour cream, handful of lettuce, three slices of tomato, 2 more Tbsp of queso fresco and finally a sprinkle of green onions.

Enjoy!

Chicken Tomatillo Enchiladas

SERVES 4

Cooking Time: 35 minutes

Nutritional Facts: Calories 559, Protein 37 g, Total Fat 25 g, Carbohydrates 49 g

Ingredients

> 1 lb fresh tomatillos, husks removed
>
> 2 chicken breast halves (bone-in)
>
> 2 tsp salt plus a pinch more
>
> ¼ cup vegetable oil
>
> 1 small onion, cut in two halves
>
> 1 cup crumbled queso fresco
>
> 5 Serrano peppers
>
> 2 cups chicken broth
>
> 1 bunch of fresh cilantro, chopped
>
> 2 cloves of garlic, divided
>
> 12 corn tortillas

Preparation Method

Place the chicken breasts in a saucepan along with one clove of garlic, 2 tsp salt and one half of onion.

Pour the broth over it.

Bring it to a boil then keep it boiling for 20 minutes.

Discard the onion and clove. Reserve the broth.

Shred the chicken with two forks. Set aside.

Combine the tomatillos and Serrano chilies in another a cooking pot. Fill it water enough the cover both the things.

Bring it to a boil and then keep it boiling till the tomatillos turns into a dull green color.

Drain the water and transfer the chilies and tomatillos to a food processor along with the other half of the onion, one clove of garlic and pinch of salt.

Add the reserved chicken broth to the processor.

Pulse till all the ingredients are thoroughly blended and pureed.

Take it out in a saucepan and bring it to a low boil.

Heat the oil in a frying pan.

When the oil is very hot, one by one fry all the tortillas in it.

Put the tortillas on a paper towel after frying, as to soak the excess oil.

Now dip the tortilla, one by one, in the low-boiling sauce.

Arrange three sauce-dipped tortillas on one serving plate.

Spoon equal amount of the shredded chicken over each tortilla.

Top up each serving with the remaining green sauce, sprinkle of crumbled cheese and finally the chopped fresh cilantro.

Enjoy!

Creamy Cheesy Chicken Enchiladas

SERVES 6 – 8

Cooking Time: 45 minutes

Nutritional Facts: Calories 252, Protein 18.3 g, Total Fat 4.6 g, Carbohydrates 35 g

Ingredients

1 cup sour cream (fat free)

7 ½ oz. canned Mexican Rotel tomatoes

16 corn tortillas

1 tbsp fresh chopped cilantro

1 medium yellow onion, diced

1 cup low fat shredded Colby-Pepper Jack Cheese

7 ½ oz. fat free cream of chicken soup (about one cup)

12 oz. cooked and shredded chicken

Cooking spray

Preparation Method

Set the oven to preheat at 350ºF.

Grease a baking dish with cooking spray.

Combine the sour cream, cilantro and soup in a saucepan.

Heat through and set aside.

Take another skillet and coat it with cooking spray.

Put the shredded chicken, onions and the Mexican rotel in the prepared skillet. Stir to mix.

Cook till the onions are translucent.

Now warm the tortillas one by one in a nonstick skillet. It will take just about a minute per side to make the tortillas warm and pliable. You can also microwave them for about 30 seconds.

Fill each tortilla with 2 Tbsp of the shredded chicken mixture and 1 Tbsp shredded cheese.

Roll up the tortilla and put it seam side down on the greased baking dish.

Spread the sour cream over the tortillas rolls and the remaining cheese.

Bake for 30 minutes, till heated through.

Enjoy!

Cheese Lovers Enchiladas

MAKES 12 enchiladas (about 6 servings)

Cooking Time: 25 minutes

Nutritional Facts: Calories 241, Protein 11.7 g, Total Fat 8.5 g, Carbohydrates 27.4 g

Ingredients

> 12 Corn Tortillas (8 inch each)
>
> Half cup reduced-fat ricotta cheese
>
> 2 Tbsp chopped green chilies
>
> Half cup cottage cheese (fat free)
>
> 19 oz. canned enchilada sauce
>
> 3 Tbsp sliced black olives
>
> 1 cup shredded Mexican four cheese blend, divided
>
> ¾ cup diced white onions
>
> Salt and pepper to taste
>
> Nonstick cooking spray

Preparation Method

Set the oven to preheat at 350°F.

Coat a casserole baking dish with cooking spray.

Now warm the tortillas one by one in a nonstick skillet. It will take just about a minute per side to make the tortillas warm and pliable. You can also microwave them for about 30 seconds.

Pour the enchilada sauce and saucepan and heat through.

Dip each tortilla in the hot enchilada sauce, shake off the dripping sauce and place the tortilla on a microwave-safe plate.

Microwave for about 30 seconds, till the tortillas are soft. Make sure the tortillas do not overlap in the plate. Do it in batches.

Set aside to cool for a while.

Now take a bowl and add in it the diced onion, cottage cheese, ricotta cheese, salt, green chilies, pepper and half of the Mexican shredded cheese. Mix well.

Fill each tortilla with about ¼ cup cheese mixture. Roll up the tortilla. Place it seam side down in the casserole dish.

Spread the remaining enchilada sauce over the rolls.

Put the dish in the preheated oven for 15 minutes.

Carefully take out the dish.

Sprinkle the remaining Mexican cheese over the enchiladas.

Top it up with black olives.

Return the dish to oven and bake for 10 more minutes.

Serve it hot!

Spicy Roasted Vegan Enchiladas with Poblano Sauce

MAKES 12 enchiladas (about 6 servings)

Cooking Time: 60 – 70 minutes

Nutritional Facts: Calories 269, Protein 9 g, Total Fat 8 g, Carbohydrates 45 g

Ingredients for Enchilada

> 3 bell peppers, (1 yellow, 1 red and 1 orange), diced
>
> ¼ tsp of salt
>
> ¾ cup chopped red onion
>
> 1 (15 oz.) can of pinto beans, rinsed
>
> Freshly ground pepper to taste
>
> 8 oz. cremini mushrooms, chopped
>
> 4½ tsp extra virgin olive oil
>
> 12 corn tortillas (6 inch each)
>
> Cooking spray

Ingredients for Poblano Sauce

> 1 poblano pepper (substitute: green bell pepper)
>
> 1 tsp salt
>
> 1 cup diced yellow onion
>
> ½ tsp chili powder
>
> ½ tsp ground cumin
>
> 8 oz. canned tomatoes, roughly diced
>
> 2 tsp extra virgin olive oil
>
> 3 cloves of garlic, minced
>
> 1 cup vegetable broth
>
> ¼ tsp paprika

Half cup fresh cilantro, coarsely chopped

Pinch of ground chipotle pepper

Preparation Method

Set the oven to preheat at 425°F.

To make the poblano sauce,

Hold the poblano with a pair of tongs. Roast it directly over the open flame while turning frequently. Roast till the pepper is evenly charred.

Place the roasted poblano pepper in a bowl.

Cover the bowl with a plastic wrap and let rest for 10 minutes.

Meanwhile, put 2 tsp oil in a saucepan and heat it over medium heat.

When the oil is hot, add the yellow onion, paprika, cumin, chipotle, chili powder and 1 tsp salt to it.

Cook and stir till the onion is soft, about 5 minutes.

Remove the pan off the heat.

Now take the poblano and peel it skins. Remove the stems and seed, and chop it.

Put the chopped poblano in the onion-containing saucepan, along with the diced tomatoes, cilantro and broth.

Return the saucepan to heat.

Cook uncovered, over medium heat for 10 – 15 minutes, till the liquid is considerably reduced and tomatoes are broken down.

Transfer it all to a food processor.

Pulse till pureed.

The poblano sauce is ready. Set aside for later use.

To make the enchiladas,

Combine the bell peppers, red onion and mushrooms in a bowl.

Arrange the vegetables in a single layer on a rimmed baking sheet.

Sprinkle the oil over the veggies.

Season with salt and pepper.

Put it in the preheated oven for 15 minutes till the veggies are soft and browned in spot. Stir the vegetables halfway in between.

Transfer all the roasted veggies to a large bowl. Stir in the pinto beans.

Reduce the temperature of the oven to 375°F.

Now take a 9x13 baking dish and spread half cup of the poblano sauce in the bottom of the dish.

Place a nonstick skillet over medium flame.

Coat both sides of a tortilla with the cooking spray and immediately place in the heated skillet. Fry the tortilla for 5 – 10 seconds per side. Likewise, fry all the tortillas.

Fill each fried tortilla with 1/3 cup of the roasted vegetable-bean mixture and 1 Tbsp of the poblano sauce.

Roll up the tortillas and arrange them seam side down in the prepared baking dish.

Spread the remaining roasted vegetable-bean mixture and poblano sauce over the rolls.

Bake, uncovered for 15 minutes

Serve it hot!

Tex Mex Green Enchiladas

MAKES 4 enchiladas (about 2 servings)

Cooking Time: 20 – 25 minutes

Nutritional Facts: Calories 335.7, Protein 29 g, Total Fat 11.4 g, Carbohydrates 31.5 g

Ingredients

> 4 whole wheat tortillas (8 inch each)
>
> 12 oz. chicken breasts, cooked and chopped
>
> ¼ cup shredded Monterey Jack cheese
>
> 1 jalapeno, seeded and minced
>
> Half cup chopped onion
>
> ¼ cup sour cream (reduced fat)
>
> 10 oz. baby spinach (about 1 lb)
>
> 1 Tbsp butter
>
> 2 Tbsp milk (fat free)
>
> 2 cups baby Portobello mushrooms, cut into slices
>
> 1 tsp cumin seeds
>
> ¼ tsp chili powder
>
> 1 (4 oz.) can of green chilies, drained and chopped
>
> Cooking spray

Preparation Method

Set the oven to preheat at 350ºF.

Combine and sour cream in a bowl. Set aside.

Heat the butter in a skillet.

When the butter starts forming bubbles, add the onion to it.

Sauté the onions for 2 minutes.

Stir in the mushrooms and sauté for 3 more minutes.

Next, stir in the jalapeno and spices. Stir to mix.

Stir in the spinach. Cook and stir till the spinach is wilted.

Add 2 Tbsp of the milk-cream mixture to the skillet. Stir to combine.

Finally, add in the chicken. Stir to combine with rest of the ingredients.

Remove the skillet off the heat.

Coat a baking dish with cooking spray.

Now soften the tortillas by putting them in the microwave for about 30 seconds or running the tortillas under cold water.

Fill each tortilla with ¾ cup of the chicken-veggie mixture.

Roll it up and place seam side down in the greased baking dish. Repeat the same with all the tortillas.

Spread the remaining chicken-veggie mixture over the rolls.

Finally, top it up the remaining milk-cream mixture, followed by cheese and then green chilies.

Bake for 15 minutes, till the cheese is melted.

Serve!

Mexican Drinks

Tequila Spiked Margarita

SERVES 4

Cooking Time: 2 minutes

Nutritional Facts: Calories 7.5, Protein 0.1 g, Total Fat 0.0 g, Carbohydrates 2.5 g

Ingredients

Half cup orange liqueur

Half cup fresh lime juice

1 cup coarsely crushed ice cubes

Half cup agave tequila

Preparation Method

Combine the lime juice, orange liqueur and tequila in a shaker.

Add ice to it. Shake for 15 seconds.

Strain in to the serving glasses.

Cheers!

Irish Choco Vodka

SERVES 4

Cooking Time: 2 minutes

Nutritional Facts: Calories 267, Protein 0.7 g, Total Fat 3.7 g, Carbohydrates 24.7 g

Ingredients

>   3 oz. Bailey's Irish Cream
>
>   6 oz. chocolate liqueur
>
>   6 oz. Kahlua
>
>   3 oz. Vodka
>
>   Coarsely cracked ice cubes

Preparation Method

Combine all the ingredients in a shaker.

Shake for 10 – 15 minutes.

Strain into wine glasses and serve!

Classic Michelada

SERVES 4

Cooking Time: 2 minutes

Nutritional Facts: Calories 242, Protein 3.1 g, Total Fat 0 g, Carbohydrates 48.5 g

Ingredients

> 1 cup cold beer
>
> 1 tsp soy sauce
>
> 2 lemons, juiced
>
> 3 cups tomato and clam juice cocktail
>
> ½ tsp salt
>
> Dash of hot pepper sauce
>
> Ice cubes

Preparation Method

Fill 4 beer mugs with ice cubes.

Spoon equal portions of soy sauce, lemon juice, salt and hot pepper sauce in each mug.

Pour equal amount of tomato and clam juice cocktail in each mug.

Top up each serving with beer. Stir gently.

You can keep topping up your mug with more beer, as you drink.

Enjoy!

Tropical Horchata

SERVES 12

Cooking Time: 5 minutes (6 hours refrigeration)

Nutritional Facts: Calories 322, Protein 7.1 g, Total Fat 17.6 g, Carbohydrates 36.5 g

Ingredients

> 1 cup white rice (uncooked)
>
> 1 (14 oz.) can of coconut milk
>
> 5 cups cold water, more if required
>
> 1 cup coconut flakes (sweetened)
>
> 1 (14 oz.) can of sweetened condensed milk
>
> 5 cups ice cubes
>
> 1 cup almonds
>
> 3 cups boiling water

Preparation Method

Combine the almonds, coconut flakes and rice in a food processor.

Process till the rice and almonds are finely ground.

Take the mixture out in a bowl.

Carefully, add the boiling water to the rice mixture.

Cover the bowl and let it rest for at least 6 hours (maximum overnight).

Transfer the mixture to a pitcher through a sieve. Make sure the liquid is completely strained of the rice and almond particles. Strain it twice if you have to.

Stir in the coconut milk and condensed milk to the sieved liquid.

Finally, stir in the cold water.

Fill each serving glass with 2 – 3 ice cubes.

Pour the horchata over ice cubes and serve!

Sunrise Horchata

SERVES 2

Cooking Time: 3 minutes

Nutritional Facts: Calories 3.8, Protein 0.0 g, Total Fat 0.0 g, Carbohydrates 1.2 g

Ingredients

> 4 oz. tequila
>
> 2 cups club soda
>
> 1 Tbsp Curacao
>
> 2 slices of lime, to garnish
>
> 1 Tbsp lime juice
>
> 2 Tbsp creme de cassis
>
> Crushed ice
>
> Ice cubes

Preparation Method

Combine the tequila, Curacao, lime juice, ice and creme de cassis in a shaker.

Shake well till combined, about 15 seconds.

Fill a tall wine glass half way with ice cubes.

Pour the drink into the glasses, through a sieve.

Top up each serving with club soda. Stir gently.

Garnish each serving with a slice of lime.

Cheers!

Hibiscus Cooler

MAKES 1 quart (about 4 servings)

Cooking Time: 15 – 20 minutes

Nutritional Facts: Calories 97.3, Protein 0.0 g, Total Fat 0.0 g, Carbohydrates 25.2 g

Ingredients

> 1 quart water
>
> 2 tsp fresh lime juice
>
> Half cup dried hibiscus flowers
>
> ½ tsp finely grated fresh ginger
>
> Half cup granulated sugar

Preparation Method

Take a saucepan and combine water and ginger in it.

Bring it to a boil over medium flame.

Turn off the heat.

Add the hibiscus flowers and sugar to the saucepan.

Let sit for 10 minutes.

Transfer the hibiscus water to a container or pitcher through a sieve.

Stir in the fresh lime juice.

Put it in the refrigerator to chill.

Enjoy!

Other Mexican Specialties

Egg and Chili Rellenos

SERVES 5 – 6

Cooking Time: 30 – 50 minutes

Nutritional Facts: Calories 263, Protein 13.1 g, Total Fat 6 g, Carbohydrates 17.3 g

Ingredients

> 2 eggs, separated
>
> 1 tsp baking powder
>
> 6 fresh Anaheim chile peppers
>
> ¾ cup all purpose flour
>
> 1 cup vegetable shortening, for frying
>
> 8 oz. queso asadero, cut into ¾ inch thick strips

Preparation Method

Adjust the oven rack at 6-inches over the heat.

Preheat the oven's broiler.

Line a baking tray with foil and place the peppers in it, at least 1 inch apart one another.

Cook the peppers under the preheated broiler for about 10 minutes, till the skin of the peppers is blackened and charred. Flip over the peppers a few times to char all sides.

Transfer the charred peppers into a bowl.

Cover the bowl with a plastic wrap. Let rest for 15 minutes.

After 15 minutes, remove the wrap and rinse the peppers with cold water to peel of their skin.

Make a slit with a sharp knife along the side of each pepper. Remove the seeds.

Rinse the peppers again, both inside and out. Pat dry.

Fill the cavity of the peppers with cheese strips.

Now take a bowl and whisk the egg yolks in it.

Whisk in the baking powder. Set aside.

Take another bowl and put the egg whites in it.

Beat the egg whites with an electric mixer till it becomes stiff.

Fold the beaten egg whites into the egg yolk mixture. Set aside.

Place the flour in a plate or shadow bowl. Set aside.

Now heat the vegetable shortening in a pan over medium flame.

Dip each cheese stuffed pepper first in flour, shake off the excess flour, then dip in the egg mixture.

Lay the coated peppers gently into the hot shortening.

Fry each side for about 5 minutes, till the cheese melts and the peppers turn lightly golden.

Serve with your favorite dip. Enjoy!

Bolillo Pork Sandwich

MAKES 6 sandwiches

Cooking Time: 3 hours

Nutritional Facts: Calories 867, Protein 47.7 g, Total Fat 41 g, Carbohydrates 75 g

Ingredients

> 10 Roma tomatoes, chopped
>
> 8 cloves of garlic, minced, plus 4 cloves more
>
> 4 ½ lbs. boneless pork butt
>
> 3 Tbsp vegetable oil
>
> 1 tsp salt
>
> Half cup water
>
> 2 dried chipotle chili peppers
>
> 2 pickled jalapeno peppers, cut into slices
>
> 1 Tbsp minced fresh oregano plus one teaspoon more
>
> 6 Mexican bolillo rolls, cut in half lengthwise and lightly toasted
>
> 1 tsp freshly ground black pepper
>
> 2 onions, diced
>
> Pinch of white sugar
>
> 2 tsp salt, and more to taste

Preparation Method

Set the oven to preheat at 475ºF.

Take a large bowl and add in it the cloves of minced garlic, 1 tablespoon oregano, pepper and 2 teaspoon salt. Mix well.

Thoroughly rub this garlic mixture over the pork butt.

Place the seasoned butt in a shallow roasting pan.

Roast the butt in the preheated oven for 20 minutes.

Now reduce the temperature of the oven to 350°F and continue roasting till the pork is tender and cooked through, about 2 hours and 15 minutes. To make sure the pork is done, insert an instant-read thermometer into the thick part of the butt. It should read 145°F.

Turn off the oven. Take the pan out it and cover it with two layers of aluminum foil.

Return the pan to the turned-off warm oven. Let rest for 20 minutes.

After 20 minutes, transfer the pork to a chopping board and chop it roughly. You can also shred it if you want. Reserve the pan drippings.

Now take a bowl and fill it with hot water.

Soak the chipotle peppers in it. Let the peppers sit in water for about 3 minutes, till softened. Drain the water. Set aside the peppers.

Now heat the vegetable oil in a nonstick skillet over medium flame.

When the oil is hot, add the 8 minced cloves to it along with diced onions.

Sauté for about 5 minutes, till the onion is soft and translucent.

Now add the roma tomatoes to it, chipotle chili pepper, sugar, 1 cup water, 5 teaspoons oregano and salt to taste. Stir to mix.

Stir in the reserved pan dripplings.

Reduce the heat to low and simmer, uncovered for 20 minutes while stirring frequently.

Allow it to cool for a while then transfer it to a food processor. Do not fill the blender pitcher more than half. Hold the lid tightly and pulse a few times to get the ingredients moving. Then pulse till it becomes a smooth puree. Transfer it to a bowl through a sieve. Repeat the same with the remaining chipotle-tomato mixture.

To make the sandwiches, spread about 2 Tbsp of the chipotle-tomato sauce over the bottom of the each roll.

Scoop equal amount of pork over the sauce in each roll.

Top up each sandwich with a few slices of pickled jalapeno.

Place the top half of the roll.

Pour about ¼ of the chipotle-tomato sauce on top of each sandwich.

Enjoy!

Spicy Bean Torta

SERVES 8

Cooking Time: 10 minutes

Nutritional Facts: Calories 354, Protein 17 g, Total Fat 9 g, Carbohydrates 60 g

Ingredients

2 whole grain baguettes (each should be 18 – 20 inches long)

30 oz. canned black beans (substitute: canned pinto beans), rinsed

2 ripe avocados, pitted

2 Tbsp fresh lime juice

2 Tbsp chopped pickled jalapeño

2 ½ cups shredded green cabbage

4 Tbsp minced onion

6 Tbsp prepared salsa

1 tsp ground cumin

Preparation Method

Combine the beans, salsa, cumin and jalapenos in a bowl. Mix well and set aside.

Take another bowl and combine the minced onion, avocado and lime in it. Mash together all the things with a potato masher.

Cut each baguette lengthwise into 4 equal parts.

Cut each part into half horizontally.

Stuff equal portions of the bean mixture between the halves of each part of the baguette, followed by the Avocado mixture and a handful of shredded cabbage.

Enjoy!

Classic Mexican Rice

SERVES 6

Cooking Time: 25 – 30 minutes

Nutritional Facts: Calories 193, Protein 4 g, Total Fat 5 g, Carbohydrates 32 g

Ingredients

> 1 ½ cups chicken broth or vegetable broth
>
> 2 Tbsp canola oil
>
> 1 Tbsp minced garlic
>
> Half cup frozen mixed vegetables, thawed
>
> Half cup finely diced onion
>
> 8 oz. canned tomato sauce (about 1 cup_
>
> 1 cup long grain white rice
>
> ¼ tsp salt

Preparation Method

First, you need a large saucepan with a tight fitting lid. Place it over medium flame.

Add oil and rice to the saucepan.

Cook and stir for about 5 minutes, till the rice begins to brown.

Stir in the salt and onion.

Cook while stirring constantly, for 2 minutes or till the onion starts to soften.

Stir in the garlic. Sauté for another minute.

Add the tomato sauce. Cook and stir for one more minute.

Finally, pour the broth in it.

Bring it to a boil. Then cover the saucepan and let it simmer for about 15 minutes, till the rice is cooked.

Stir in the mixed vegetables.

Heat through and serve!

Mexican Flavored Drunken Tilapia

SERVES 8

Cooking Time: 30 – 40 minutes

Nutritional Facts: Calories 120, Protein 11 g, Total Fat 6 g, Carbohydrates 4 g

Ingredients

> 1 ¼ lbs tilapia, cut into 2-inch long and half inch thin strips
>
> ¾ cup beer
>
> ¼ tsp dried oregano
>
> ¼ cup whole wheat pastry flour
>
> ¼ tsp dry mustard
>
> ¼ tsp freshly ground black pepper
>
> Half cup all purpose flour
>
> ½ tsp salt
>
> 3 Tbsp canola oil, divided
>
> ¼ tsp cayenne pepper

Preparation Method

Combine the beer, salt, all purpose flour, oregano, cayenne pepper, whole wheat flour, mustard and black pepper in a food processor.

Blend till it is smooth, stopping occasionally to scrape down the sides.

Transfer it all to a shallow dish.

Toss fish in it. Turn to coat all sides.

Now take a large nonstick skillet and heat 1 Tbsp canola oil in it.

When the oil is hot, place one-third of the coated fish in it

Fry till the fish is golden brown, for about 4 minutes per side.

Take it out to a plate. Keep warm.

Add another 1 Tbsp of canola to the skillet.

When the oil is hot, place half of the remaining fish to it.

Cook till golden brown, 3 – 4 minutes per side.

Take it out in the same plate. Keep warm.

Repeat the same with the remaining oil and fish.

Serve immediately with any of your favorite dip.

Enchilada Corn Casserole

SERVES 8 – 10

Cooking Time: 35 – 40 minutes

Nutritional Facts: Calories 243, Protein 9 g, Total Fat 10 g, Carbohydrates 30 g

Ingredients

> 12 corn tortillas, quartered
>
> 1 Tbsp canola oil
>
> 14 oz. canned diced tomatoes, drained
>
> 1 medium sized zucchini, grated
>
> 1 teaspoon ground cumin
>
> 1 ½ cups fresh corn or frozen corns (thawed)
>
> 19 oz. canned green enchilada sauce
>
> 1 medium sized onion, chopped
>
> 19 oz. canned black beans, rinsed
>
> 1 ¼ cups shredded Cheddar cheese (reduced fat)
>
> ½ tsp salt
>
> Cooking spray

Preparation Method

Set the oven to preheat at 400°F.

Grease a 9x13 baking dish with cooking spray.

Place a large nonstick skillet over medium-high flame. Heat the canola oil in it.

When the oil is hot, add chopped onion to it.

Sauté for about 5 minutes or till the onion starts to brown.

Add beans, zucchini, corn, salt, cumin and tomatoes to the onions in the skillet.

Cook for 3 minutes while stirring occasionally.

Spread half of the tortilla quarters in the prepared baking dish.

Spread half of the vegetable mixture over the tortillas.

Top it up with half of the enchilada sauce, followed by half of the cheese.

Arrange the second layer of tortillas over cheese.

Top it up with the remaining vegetables, enchilada sauce and finally the cheese.

Cover the dish with aluminum foil.

Put it in the preheated oven for 15 minutes.

Remove the foil and continue baking for another 10 minutes, till the casserole bubbles around the edges.

Serve it hot!

Tex Mex Tostadas

SERVES 4

Cooking Time: 30 – 35 minutes

Nutritional Facts: Calories 397, Protein 33 g, Total Fat 15 g, Carbohydrates 34 g

Ingredients

1 (14 oz.) can of petite diced tomatoes with jalapeños, undrained

2 Tbsp chopped fresh cilantro

1 avocado, pitted

2 Tbsp sour cream (reduced fat)

12 oz. shredded cooked chicken or turkey (about 3 cups)

1 medium sized onion, cut into thin slices

1 cup shredded romaine lettuce

8 corn tortillas

Half cup shredded Monterey Jack cheese

¼ cup prepared salsa

Cooking spray

Preparation Method

Set the oven to preheat at 375°F.

Empty the can of petite diced tomatoes with jalapeños in saucepan.

Bring it to a boil over medium flame.

Add the onions to it.

Cook for 15 – 20 minutes, till the onion is soft and almost all the liquid is evaporated. Stir occasionally.

Stir in the shredded chicken or turkey. Stir to combine and heat through, about 2 minutes.

Now coat both sides of the tortillas with cooking spray.

Lay the tortillas in one large baking sheet.

Bake for 10 about minutes, till the tortillas are light brown and crispy. Turn once in between. You can also bake in batches if you don't have a large baking sheet.

Place the avocado in a bowl and mash it with potato masher.

Stir in the salsa, cilantro and sour cream. Mix well.

To make the tostadas, spread equal amount of the avocado mixture over each tortilla.

Top it up with the chicken mixture followed by a handful of lettuce and a sprinkle of cheese.

Enjoy!

Turkey Mexican Cheese Calzone

SERVES 4

Cooking Time: 20 – 25 minutes

Nutritional Facts: Calories 414, Protein 47.7 g, Total Fat 14 g, Carbohydrates 29 g

Ingredients

> 1 lb. extra lean ground turkey
>
> 1 ½ tsp chili powder
>
> ¾ cup salsa verde (fire roasted)
>
> 2 cloves of garlic, minced
>
> 1 cup shredded Mexican blend cheese
>
> Half cup finely chopped red bell pepper
>
> Half cup finely chopped onion
>
> 1 egg white, beaten
>
> ¾ tsp ground cumin
>
> 1 (11 oz.) can of frozen pizza dough (thin crust)

Preparation Method

Set the oven to preheat at 425ºF.

Position the rack of the oven to the top third slot.

Place a large nonstick skillet over medium - high flame.

When then skillet is hot, add the turkey to it.

Cook and stir for 5 minutes.

Stir in the garlic and onion.

Cook and stir for about 5 more minutes, till the onions become soft and translucent.

Stir in the cumin and chili powder. Cook for another minute.

Add the bell peppers. Cook and stir for one more minute.

Remove the skillet off the heat. Stir in the salsa. Set aside.

Now unroll the dough and divide it into 4 equal parts.

Working with one dough rectangle at a time, scoop half cup of the turkey mixture on the right half of the dough.

Top it up with 2 Tbsp of cheese.

Now brush the beaten egg white on the edges of the pizza dough.

Fold the left half of the dough over the turkey filling.

Press a fork to seal. Brush a bit of egg white over the top to make the crust crispy.

Repeat the same with the remaining dough, turkey and cheese.

Bake it for about 12 minutes, till golden brown.

Enjoy!

Hot and Sour Salmon Tostadas

SERVES 4

Cooking Time: 15 – 20 minutes

Nutritional Facts: Calories 319, Protein 16 g, Total Fat 11 g, Carbohydrates 43 g

Ingredients

15 oz. canned black beans, rinsed

8 corn tortillas (6 inch each)

2 cups shredded cabbage

2 scallions, diced

2 Tbsp chopped fresh cilantro

3 Tbsp sour cream (reduced fat)

1 avocado, pitted and diced

1 (7 oz.) can of wild Alaskan salmon (boneless and skinless), drained

2 Tbsp prepared salsa

2 Tbsp minced jalapenos (pickled) plus 2 Tbsp pickle juice, divided

Cooking spray

Preparation Method

Set the oven to preheat at 375°F.

Take a bowl and combine the salmon, jalapenos and avocado in it. Set aside.

Take another bowl and combine cilantro, cabbage and pickle juice in it. Set aside.

Now place the black beans in a food processor along with the salsa, sour cream and scallions.

Pulse till it is smooth.

Pour it out in a microwave resistant bowl.

Cover the bowl and put it in the microwave, for 2 minutes on high heat. Set aside.

Now coat both sides of the tortillas with cooking spray.

Lay the tortillas in one large baking sheet.

Bake for 10 about minutes, till the tortillas are light brown and crispy. Turn once in between. You can also bake in batches if you don't have a large baking sheet.

To make the tostadas, spread equal amount of the black beans paste over each tortilla.

Top up each tortilla with equal portions of the salmon mixture followed by a sprinkle of the cabbage-cilantro mixture.

Enjoy!

Corn and Chili Casseroles

SERVES 4

Cooking Time: 25 – 35 minutes

Nutritional Facts: Calories 215, Protein 23 g, Total Fat 7 g, Carbohydrates 14 g

Ingredients

> 8 oz. canned diced green chiles, drained and pat dry
>
> 1½ cup milk (fat free)
>
> 4 large eggs
>
> 4 scallions, cut into thin slices
>
> 6 large egg whites
>
> ¼ tsp salt
>
> ¾ cup frozen corns, thawed and pat dry
>
> 1 cup shredded Cheddar cheese (low fat)
>
> Cooking spray

Preparation Method

Set the oven to preheat at 400°F.

Coat 8 (6 oz. each) heat proof ramekins with cooking spray. You can also use 4 (10 oz. each) ramekins.

Place all the prepared ramekins on a baking sheet.

Spoon equal amount of green chiles, corns and scallions in each ramekin

Top up each with cheese.

Combine the milk, eggs, salt and egg whites in a bowl. Whisk well.

Pour equal portions of the egg mixture in each ramekin.

Put it in the preheated oven, till the eggs are set and the tops begin to brown, about 25 minutes for 6 oz. ramekins and 35 minutes if you are using 10 oz. ramekins.

Serve it hot!

Mexican Shrimp Delight

SERVES 8

Cooking Time: 10 – 15 minutes

Nutritional Facts: Calories 192, Protein 24 g, Total Fat 6 g, Carbohydrates 11 g

Ingredients

2 lbs raw shrimp (18 – 20 shrimps per pound), peeled and deveined

4 tsp canola oil

8 cloves of garlic, minced

6 medium sized tomatoes, diced

2 medium sized onion, cut into thin slices

Half cup green olives, pitted and thinly sliced

2 bay leaves

2 jalapeno peppers, remove the seeds and cut into thin slices

Lime wedges, for garnishing

Preparation Method

Place a large nonstick pan over medium flame and heat oil int.

When the oil is hot, add bay leaves to it. Cook for 1 minute.

Stir in the jalapenos, onion and garlic. Sauté for about 3 minutes till the veggies are soft.

Add shrimps to the pan.

Cover the pan and let it cook for 4 – 5 minutes, till the shrimps are just cooked through.

Add the olives and tomatoes to the shrimps.

Reduce the flame to medium-low and simmer uncovered for about 3 minutes, till the tomatoes are broken down.

Discard the bay leaves.

Garnish with lime wedges and serve!

Mexican Sweet Delights

Apple Pie Tortillas

SERVES 6

Cooking Time: 20 minutes

Nutritional Facts: Calories 484, Protein 4.5 g, Total Fat 13.5 g, Carbohydrates 88.3 g

Ingredients

21 oz. canned apple pie filling

Half cup white sugar

1 tsp ground cinnamon

Half cup water

6 flour tortillas (8 inch each)

1/3 cup margarine

Half cup packed brown sugar

Cooking spray

Preparation Method

Set the oven to preheat at 350°F.

Coat an 8x8 baking dish with cooking spray.

Divide the apple pie filling equally among all tortillas. Place it in the centre of the tortilla followed by a sprinkle of cinnamon.

Roll up the tortillas and place them seam side down on the prepared baking dish.

Combine the margarine, water and sugar in saucepan.

Bring it to a boil over medium flame.

Reduce the heat to simmer and cook for 3 minutes, while stirring constantly.

Pour the sauce over the tortillas.

Sprinkle a pinch of extra cinnamon over the sauce.

Put it in the preheated oven for 20 minutes.

Enjoy!

Sopapilla Cream Cheese Delight

MAKES 1 (9x13 inches) cheesecake, (10 – 12 servings)

Cooking Time: 45 minutes

Nutritional Facts: Calories 553, Protein 7.4 g, Total Fat 36 g, Carbohydrates 50 g

Ingredients

24 oz. cream cheese, softened

Half cup melted butter

1 ½ tsp vanilla extract

1 tsp ground cinnamon

2 cups white sugar, divided

¼ cup sliced almonds

2 (8 oz. each) cans of crescent roll dough

Preparation Method

Set the oven to preheat at 350ºF.

Combine the cream cheese, 1 ½ cups of sugar and vanilla extract in a bowl. Beat till smooth.

Unroll the dough.

Use a rolling pin to press the dough and shape each piece into a 9x13 inches rectangle.

Press one piece in the base of a 9x13 inches baking dish.

Pour the cream mixture over it and spread it evenly with a spatula.

Cover it up with the second piece of the dough.

Spread the melted butter evenly on top of the second dough.

Mix the remaining sugar with cinnamon in a bowl, and sprinkle it over the cheesecake.

Finally, drizzle with the sliced almonds.

Put it in the preheated oven for about 45 minutes, till the dough is puffed and golden brown.

Allow it to cool for a while.

Slice and serve!

Drunken Margarita Cake

MAKES 1 (10 inches) Bundt cake, (10 – 12 servings)

Cooking Time: 45 – 50 minutes

Nutritional Facts: Calories 393, Protein 4 g, Total Fat 16 g, Carbohydrates 53.7 g

Ingredients for Cake

1 (18 ½ oz.) box of orange cake mix

2/3 cup water

4 eggs

¼ cup tequila

¼ cup fresh lemon juice

1 (3.4 oz.) box of instant vanilla pudding mix

2 Tbsp triple sec liqueur

Half cup vegetable oil

Ingredients for Glaze

1 cup confectioners' sugar

2 Tbsp triple sec liqueur

2 Tbsp lime juice

1 Tbsp tequila

Preparation Method

Set the oven to preheat at 350ºF.

Now take a 10 inch Bundt pan. Grease and flour it.

Combine the orange cake mix, eggs, lemon juice, vanilla pudding mix, oil, tequila, water and triple sec in a bowl. Beat for 2 minutes with a electric beater.

Transfer the batter to the prepared Bundt pan.

Put it in the preheated oven for 45 – 50 minutes or till a toothpick when inserted in the middle of the cake comes out clean.

Meanwhile make the glaze.

To make the glaze, combine all glaze ingredients in a bowl. Whisk till smooth.

When the cake is done, turn off the oven and let the cake cool in the pan for 10 minutes.

Take it out in the cake rack and drizzle with the glaze while the cake is still warm.

Slice and serve!

Tres Leches Delight

SERVES 7 – 8

Cooking Time: 45 – 50 minutes

Nutritional Facts: Calories 642, Protein 14.2 g, Total Fat 33 g, Carbohydrates 75 g

Ingredients

1 (14 oz.) can of sweetened condensed milk

1 cup white sugar, divided

1 tsp vanilla extract

1 ½ tsp baking powder

5 egg whites

10 maraschino cherries

1 cup all purpose flour

1 (12 fl oz.) can of evaporated milk

5 egg yolks

1 pint of heavy whipping cream, divided

1/3 cup milk

Preparation Method

Set the oven to preheat at 350°F.

Grease and flour a 9 inch springform pan.

Take a large bowl and add in it the egg yolks and ¾ cup of sugar.

Beat till it is almost double in volume.

Fold in the flour, vanilla extract milk and baking powder. Set aside.

Take another bowl and place the egg whites in it. Beat till it a soft peaks form.

Gradually add the remaining sugar while beating constantly. Continue beating till it is firm but not very dry.

Fold the beaten egg whites into the egg yolk mixture.

Pour the batter evenly into the prepared springform pan.

Put it in the preheated oven for 45 – 50 minutes or till a toothpick when inserted in the middle of the cake comes out clean.

Let it cool in the pan for 10 minutes.

Loosen the edges of the cake with a knife.

Allow it to cool completely and then take it out in the serving plate or rack.

Use a cake tester or a two prong fork to pierce the top of the cake.

Take a bowl and combine the evaporated milk, condensed milk and ¼ cup of the whipping cream in it. Mix well.

Take out one cup from it. Discard or reserve for later use.

Spread the remaining milk mixture over the cake. Pour it slowly and gradually, till all of it is absorbed by the cake.

Whip the remaining whipping cream till it achieves a spreadable consistency.

Frost the cake with the whipped cream.

Garnish with maraschino cherries.

Serve!

Classic Mexican Fritters

SERVES 8

Cooking Time: 10 – 15 minutes

Nutritional Facts: Calories 691, Protein 3.3 g, Total Fat 51 g, Carbohydrates 57 g

Ingredients

> 2 cups water
>
> 4 Tbsp vegetable oil
>
> 1 cup powdered more
>
> 2 cups all purpose flour
>
> 5 Tbsp white sugar
>
> 2 tsp ground cinnamon
>
> 1 tsp salt
>
> 4 quarts of oil, for frying

Preparation Method

Combine the water, 5 Tbsp sugar, 4 Tbsp vegetable oil and salt in saucepan.

Bring it to a boil over medium flame.

Fold in the flour. Knead.

Fill it in a pastry bag.

Place the oil in a deep fryer and heat it to 375ºF.

Pipe out strips of the dough into the hot oil

Fry till the churros are golden brown.

Absorb the excess oil on paper towels.

Combine the remaining sugar and cinnamon in a shallow plate or dish.

Toss the fried churros in it. Roll to coat.

Enjoy!

Traditional Biscochitos

Makes about 72 cookies (6 dozen)

Cooking Time: 10 minutes

Nutritional Facts: Calories 113, Protein 1.3 g, Total Fat 6 g, Carbohydrates 13 g

Ingredients

> 6 cups all purpose flour, sifted
>
> 1 Tbsp ground cinnamon
>
> 1 ½ cups white sugar plus ¼ cup more
>
> ¼ tsp salt
>
> 2 eggs
>
> 2 tsp anise seed
>
> 2 Tbsp baking powder
>
> 2 cups lard
>
> ¼ cup brandy

Preparation Method

Set the oven to preheat at 350ºF.

Combine the sifted flour, salt and baking powder in a bowl. Mix well and set aside.

Take another large bowl and combine the lard and 1 ½ cups sugar in it. Beat till smooth.

Stir in the anise seed.

Beat till it becomes fluffy.

Start adding eggs to it. Add one egg at a time and beat after every addition.

Fold the flour mixture in it.

Finally, stir in the brandy.

Using a rolling pin, roll out the dough to ¼ thick. Do this on a floured surface.

Cut it into desired cookie shapes.

Place the cookies onto the baking sheet, at least one inch apart one another.

Combine the extra ¼ cup sugar and cinnamon in a bowl, and sprinkle it over the cookies.

Bake the cookies for about 10 minutes, or till the bottoms are lightly browned.

Enjoy the fresh homemade Mexican style cookies!

Keep the cookies in an airtight container.

Tortilla Pear Delight

SERVES 6

Cooking Time: 10 – 15 minutes

Nutritional Facts: Calories 746, Protein 9 g, Total Fat 35 g, Carbohydrates 104 g

Ingredients

6 flour tortillas (8 inch each)

4 Bartlett pears, core the pears and dice them

1 tsp lemon rind

1 quart of vanilla ice cream

1 Tbsp cornstarch

¼ cup honey

Half cup graham crackers (crumbled)

Half cup white sugar

2 tsp ground cinnamon, divided

1 quart of vegetable oil, to fry the tortillas

Half cup chopped pecans

Preparation Method

Place the vegetable oil in a deep fryer and heat it to 375°F.

When the oil is hot, put one flour tortilla in it. Immediately press the center of the tortilla gently with a spoon. Keep pressing the spoon in the center till the tortilla takes the shape of a cup. Likewise, fry all the other tortillas.

Now take a saucepan and combine the pears, cornstarch, 1 tsp ground cinnamon, sugar and lemon zest in it.

Bring it to a boil over medium flame while stirring constantly.

Keep it boiling for a minute longer.

Allow it to cool.

Now take a bowl and put in it the cookie crumbs, the remaining 1 tsp cinnamon and pecans. Mix well and set aside.

Brush each tortilla cup with honey.

Divide the vanilla ice cream into 6 equal parts and form a ball of each part.

Roll out the ice cream balls in the cookie-pecan mixture, and then scoop each ball into the prepared tortilla cups.

Top up each cup with equal amount of the pear mixture.

Serve immediately!

Printed in Great Britain
by Amazon.co.uk, Ltd.,
Marston Gate.